According to His Word: A 31 – Day Devotional for Entrepreneurs

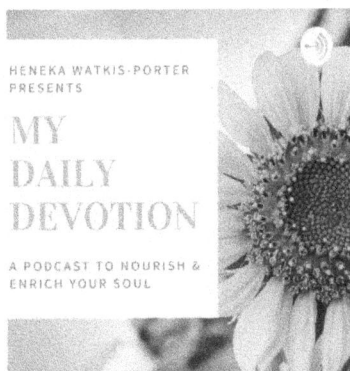

HENEKA WATKIS-PORTER PRESENTS

MY DAILY DEVOTION

A PODCAST TO NOURISH & ENRICH YOUR SOUL

Listen to this FREE podcast by Heneka Watkis-Porter. My Daily Devotion is available in iTunes and everywhere else podcasts are found.

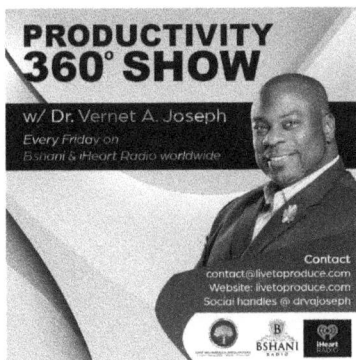

PRODUCTIVITY 360° SHOW

w/ Dr. Vernet A. Joseph

Every Friday on
Bshani & iHeart Radio worldwide

Contact
contact@livetoproduce.com
Website: livetoproduce.com
Social handles @ drvajoseph

BSHANI RADIO

Listen to this FREE podcast by Dr. Vernet A. Joseph. Productivity 360 is available in iTunes and everywhere else podcasts are found.

DR. VERNET A. JOSEPH
HENEKA WATKIS-PORTER

PUBLISHED BY Live To Produce Publishing Group

ISBN- 13: 978-0-9968628-8-2

ISBN-10: 0-9968628-8-9

WHAT OTHERS ARE SAYING ABOUT HENEKA WATKIS-PORTER & HER WORK

Heneka's objective is to prove to young and aspiring businesspersons that like her, who began life with so many disadvantages, they can dream big and realize their goals.

His Excellency the Most Honourable Sir Patrick L. Allen, ON, GCMG, CD
Governor-General of Jamaica

Heneka's energy and passion shine though in every Podcast episode. She extracts value bombs from her guests and shares priceless information with her audience. She is truly ON FIRE!

John Lee Dumas of Entrepreneurs on Fire

"This book (15 Hints to Entrepreneurial Success) is a 'must-read' for anyone who is an entrepreneur or wishes to be one. Read this book and you will certainly be inspired and motivated to be the owner of your own business and inevitably, to lead your own life!"

Lisanne Chai-Hamilton
ActionCoach Entrepreneur of the Year, The Stationery Centre

WHAT OTHERS ARE SAYING ABOUT DR. VERNET A. JOSEPH, HIS WORK

Dr. Vernet, will help you to begin to expand your mind and encourage you to see that you can do more than you ever imagined. He states "Your dream is possible" a message that is needed now more than ever before. Listen to Dr. Vernet, it will change your life."

Les Brown,
Worlds #1 Motivational Speaker, The Les Brown Institute

Dr. Vernet Alin Joseph, your work and strategies have a tremendous impact on the lives of many people daily, helping them to have a positive and productive impact on the lives of many others in the day, weeks and years to come.

Tasha "TC" Cooper,
Founder of UpwardActionMedia® and
FaithFocusFlow™

I was absolutely blown away from attending one of Dr. Vernet Joseph's events. I travel all around the world doing events and I can tell you unequivocally, that the organization, speakers and content that he brings to his events and engagements are life changing. Dr. Joseph, thank you for being the man that you are, being as caring as you are, and being as committed to helping people take their business and lives to the next level. We need more people like you.

Dr. Ruben West,
Founder of Black Belt Speakers, Published Author,
Success Coach and Trainer.

Dr. Vernet is the leading authority in productivity around the world. He speaks, trains and teaches on the topic masterfully. I have watched this man make a difference and change the lives of everyone who he encounters. All I can say is you are a class act my friend. Thank you for putting on truly unbelievable events with Golden Rule awards and Productive Business Summit.

Ambassador Dr. Clyde Rivers,
Founder of IChangeNations™

INSPIRE & INFLUENCE OTHERS!
"Share This Book"

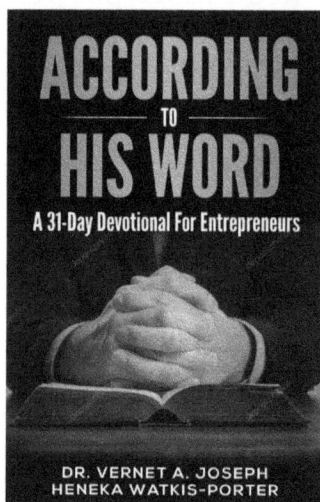

ACCORDING
TO
HIS WORD
A 31-Day Devotional For Entrepreneurs

DR. VERNET A. JOSEPH
HENEKA WATKIS-PORTER

Retail $19.99

Special Quantity Discounts

5-20 Books	$17.99
21-99 Books	$15.99
100-499 Books	$13.99
500-999 Books	$8.99
1,000+ Books	$6.99

To Place an Order Contact:
(480) 331-8482
contact@Livetoproduce.com
www.Livetoproduce.com

DEDICATION

All around us every day are things to distract us from our purpose. This devotional is dedicated to you because you have chosen to live on purpose. It is intended to guide you into moments of reflection, acknowledging God as your source of life and livelihood, as you continue on your entrepreneurial journey.

THE IDEAL PROFESSIONAL SPEAKERS
FOR YOUR NEXT EVENT!

Any organization that wants to develop their
people to become *'extraordinarily productive'*
needs to hire Dr. Vernet A. Joseph & Heneka
Watkis-Porter for speaking engagements such as:
Keynotes, Trainings and Workshops.

TO CONTACT/BOOK DR. VERNET OR
HENEKA TO SPEAK:

Dr. Vernet contactliveproduce@gmail.com
Heneka henekawatkisporter@gmail.com

INTRODUCTION

You were born to dominate and rule over this Earth. You already have everything that is required to make you successful as you pursue your life's purpose. But do you know it? The Bible reminds us that it is for a lack of knowledge that the people perish. According to His Word is a devotional that teaches you about God's Word and how to leverage it to win in life.

As an entrepreneur, you are often faced with a myriad of challenges every day. Some days seem to cruise on auto-pilot, while on other days you can't help but wonder if it is possible for anything else to go wrong. As you read and meditate each day, you will be able to reflect on what it means to live in gratitude; increase your faith; develop a productive mindset; remain diligent and so much more.

Each day, *According to His Word* gives you a relevant scripture, followed by an encouraging word, and ends with a prayer for the day. You will be taken on a journey of faith and serenity as you become emboldened to continue on an entrepreneurial path. For example, on Day 6 where the devotional addresses being of 'Power, love and a sound mind', it entreats you to make a decision to *"grab the bull by the horns and do what is right according to God's will and purpose for your life".*

The authors, Heneka Watkis-Porter and Dr. Vernet A. Joseph, draw on their experiences from a Christian, and entrepreneurial perspective to help you to live victoriously and guided by Christ. For example, Heneka shares about when she contemplated quitting her nine to five to start her own business and how Colossians 3:23 became relevant to her. She was convicted of the need to work as though she was working for God. This wasn't happening in her job and she wanted to change that by giving full attention to what she loved so that her heart could be fully in it.

As a 'productivity evangelist', Dr. Vernet brings a unique perspective to the devotional from his experience gained from the military. On Day 28, "Live to Produce", he reminds us that, *"we were created to bring him (God) glory by doing exactly what he has already intended for us to do".*

If you are looking to learn more about your God-given purpose and how to become more productive, *According to His Word* is for you.

TABLE OF CONTENTS

DAY
ONE

WORKING WITH ALL YOUR HEART

WORKING WITH ALL YOUR HEART

Day 1: Working with all Your Heart
Colossians 3:23

Whatever you do, work at it with all your heart, as working for the Lord, not for human masters.

I (Heneka) recall years ago I contemplated, deliberated and agonized over whether I should quit my permanent, secure job to become a full-time entrepreneur. This passage saved me. I was working with an organization that was the envy of many; gainfully employed but extremely discontented.

As I reflected on the plans God had for my life, I eventually realized that I wasn't pleasing Him. I was working, but not unto God; I was unfulfilled. There was no joy and inner peace with what I was doing – although I remember time and again expressing gratitude for the blessing of having a job.

I wasn't giving my job my all when I really should.

When we find that we are doing things from a place other than that of joy, we need to confess it ask of God to change our mindset to a positive one while we do our part in finding a solution to our happiness.

God doesn't want us to merely exist, going through the motion just to get by. He wants us to thrive and that is why he requires us to live on purpose.

Purpose fuels us to get up each day knowing that we are about to do what we are truly meant to do.

Ultimately, we are to impact lives, making it better for our families, communities, world and ourselves – that pleases God.

Prayer: Father I thank you for my life. I thank you that I am fearfully and wonderfully made. I know you have great plans for my life. I pray that I will be purposeful in everything that I do. I want to align with your word to do everything from my heart so that you can bless it. In Jesus' name. Amen.

DAY
TWO

PROFIT FROM YOUR PLANS

PROFIT FROM YOUR PLANS

Day 2: Profit From Your Plans
Proverbs 21:5

The plans of the diligent lead to profit as surely as haste leads to poverty.

Entrepreneurs are by nature, risk-takers. This can sometimes lead to hasty decisions without proper planning.

Sometimes we fail to plan because of our very state of mind which run counter to having a life of success. Poverty of thought - a state where persons keep returning to the same limiting beliefs - is worse than the lack of material possessions. It is our thoughts that manifest into things. Whatever we give attention to, gets magnified.

To accomplish anything of worth, we must understand that success isn't magic, happening all on its own. A precondition for victory is strategic planning.

But it takes a diligent person to set specific, measurable, attainable, realistic and time-bound goals. Not only should we set them, but also stick to them. Our targets should also be exciting and specifically related to our season.

We may know of the five second rule (the longer it takes to act from the stage of ideation to execution), the more likely it is that there will be no action at all. This rule, when taken against the backdrop of a foundational plan, will help us to achieve our goals.

His word reminds us that when our ways please him, he will 'grant us the desires of our hearts.'

When we seek God continuously in whatever we do, He will guide us and allow resources to come into our path to achieve our goals.

Prayer: Dear God, I commit my plans to you for success. In the moments when I'm tempted to make hasty decisions without your sanctioning, reign me in so that everything that I do can be pleasing to you. In Jesus' name. Amen.

DAY
THREE

BE A GENEROUS GIVER

BE A GENEROUS GIVER

Day 3: Be a Generous Giver
Psalm 112:5

Good will come to those who are generous and lend freely, who conduct their affairs with justice.

There are many irrefutable laws of life. The law of sowing and reaping, a powerful force that governs our success as entrepreneurs, is one of them. When you give to others, you are sowing into their lives and the ripple effect is tremendous.

Have you ever reflected on how you felt after extending a helping hand to someone in need of your time, talent or finances? It is certainly more blessed to give than to receive.

When you combine your faith in the Word of God with your giving, you will begin to experience success beyond your imagination. If you struggle to be a giver, prayerfully seek God to soften your heart to extend to those who need you. In our humanity, we sometimes want to withhold things of value from others, but His word reminds us that when we seek Him first and His righteousness, everything that we need will be given to us.

This truth will allow us to shift the way we see giving. In our open-handedness, it is our best that we should present. This will position us to reap God's best.

We should reach out to others unconditionally. When it's time for our harvesting, we will reap what we sow. What we give, comes right back in a much more exponential way than how we expect and from whom we expect.

Prayer: Yahweh, you are my shepherd which means you will always take care of me. I don't have to withhold my resources as you are my provider, and all good things come from you. Thank you for placing in me, a heart to give. Help me to give without expecting anything in return. In Jesus' name. Amen.

DAY
FOUR

DELIGHT YOURSELF IN GOD

DELIGHT YOURSELF IN GOD

Day 4: Delight Yourself in God
Psalm 37:4

Take delight in the Lord, and he will give you the desires of your heart.

We all have a deep yearning for many things that we believe will give us joy. This is a matter of choice and preference for each person. What remains constant for all, is that a close walk with God will lead to fulfillment even beyond what we thought possible.

Sometimes it's the little things of getting that parking space that is closer to your meeting place; it could be coming home to see that your spouse prepared your favorite meal after you've been longing for it all day or even have someone allowing you to go ahead of them in the line at the bank so that you wouldn't miss your child's football game.

When we take conscious note of what God expects of us, the desires that arise from the deepest recesses of our innermost being flow from him. It is his will to see us prosper even as our souls prosper.

But what does it really mean to delight in God, you may ask? It is abiding in his word; having daily communication with him, praying without ceasing. This doesn't mean that you are constantly on your knees physically. Instead, it requires an eternal conscious awareness of who you are as a child of God, what your purpose is and that you've been wonderfully and fearfully made by him for his purpose. This leads you to live a life grounded in gratitude. When you are grateful for what you now have, you are saying to God that he can trust you with more.

Want the things your heart desire? Delight in God.

Prayer: Abba, thank you for creating me with desires so that I can enjoy your creation here on earth. I pray that I will walk with you daily in a way that pleases you. Help me to desire only the things that are aligned to your will for my life. Take away my desire for anything that is not of you. In Jesus' name, Amen.

DAY
FIVE

ALL THINGS WORK FOR GOOD

ALL THINGS WORK FOR GOOD

Day 5: All Things Work for Good
Romans 8:28

All things work together for good for they that love the Lord and are called according to his purpose.

It took me a while to truly appreciate this scripture. It wasn't until my late 20's when I became fully aware and appreciative of what it means. It is now one of my favorites. I came to recognize that while not all things are good, all things work for good in the Lord.

Entrepreneurship by its very definition is 'risky business'. As long as there is a potential for the risk of something not going in your favor, there will be days when everything seemingly goes south.

That is why having a clear purpose on your entrepreneurial journey is very important. It is this 'why' that will keep you going when the going gets tough. The challenges are meant to strengthen your muscle, preparing you to take on projects with far more impact than what you had initially envisioned.

The more difficult situations in all spheres of your life (business, professional, personal, relational, etc.), will teach life lessons that will lead to a good outcome and increased faith.

Sometimes it seems God is absent in a crisis. But as you know, very rarely is the teacher present in a test session. He or she has already prepared you for such situation. The teacher can be confident knowing that you will do your best.

The next challenge you face, ask yourself this question, *"if I knew that all my issues will be resolved when I wake up tomorrow, would I still worry?"*

Whatever it is that you face, tell yourself that it will all be gone tomorrow – even if tomorrow is a year from now. What doesn't kill you will always make you stronger.

Prayer: Heavenly Father, you are all knowing and because of this you can see at the end of my challenges. You have allowed the challenges to come to me so I can extend my faith in you.

Remind me always that all things are working together for my good. In Jesus' name. Amen.

DAY
SIX

POWER, LOVE AND A SOUND MIND

POWER, LOVE AND A SOUND MIND

Day 6: Power, Love and a Sound Mind
2 Timothy 1:7

For the Spirit God gave us does not make us timid, but gives us power, love and self-discipline.

When was the last time you had a really great idea that you know would be a hit if you decided to pursue it? You've visualized what executing on it would mean for you, your family and your community. Yet the voices in your head talked you out of it.

We've all experienced this unpleasant feeling about the threat of danger and peril whether real or imagined. It is called fear. This crippling emotion is not of God. Whenever we feel that way, we must remind ourselves of what the word of God says.

Our Creator is love and love casts out all fear. Let the love of God dwells deeply within you. It is this love that empowers you to be your best self. Don't cheat others of the awesome leader you are by holding back from them what only you can give. You are called to dominate your circumstances. Live boldly, be confident as you have been given everything you need for your success, but you first have to believe it.

Decide to grab the bull by the horns and do what is right according to God's will and purpose for your life. Let love reign within you instead of allowing fear to take root.

Prayer: Mighty God, because of you I can step boldly into my authority. I pray that any hint of fear may be eradicated from my life. Allow me to face my fears with confidence in who you are. Let your love for me take precedence over any other emotions. In Jesus' name. Amen.

DAY
SEVEN

ASK, SEEK, KNOCK

ASK, SEEK, KNOCK

Day 7: Ask, Seek, Knock
Matthew 7:7

Ask and it will be given to you; seek and you will find; knock and the door will be opened to you.

If ever you felt bashful about asking God for anything, this scripture is a blunt reminder that you shouldn't. Not only should we ask our all-knowing Creator for the things that we need to see manifested in our lives, we ought to ask of others what we expect them to do for us.

If you lack wisdom, knowledge and understanding, ask of God to open your eyes, ears and heart to receive that which he wants to pour into you.

We must seek out that which we desire and knock on some doors to get answers. This is telling us that we have to be intentional in pursuing our goals. It is not about wishful thinking, but deliberate, decisive action taken on our path for our success.

Entrepreneurship is about a relentless pursuit of that vision that God has placed in our hearts. We have to be hungry enough to see it through till the end even in the midst of uncertainty and challenges.

God wants us to shine brightly in our calling. Our accomplishment is a testimony to the world that God is on our side. Let us arise each day with this knowledge. It will give us the confidence to unashamedly and enthusiastically ask, seek and knock.

When we ask, seek and knock, the answers may not come in the time that we want them to. This also helps to teach us patience. The things we never get, are the things that weren't meant for us.

We are reminded to be patient in the process of waiting. Many times, we think only of the end and discount the different U-turns and roundabouts that we inevitable face along the way. It is part of the journey and we should enjoy it because every part of it is important.

Never discount the value of your set-backs; embrace them as part of the process and allow God to take you through them.

Prayer: Jehovah Jireh, you are my provider. You have given me the grace for my success. You want me to shine so that others can know that you are real. Let me always allow my light to be brightly burning for you. Remind me to seek you first in everything that applies to my life. Give me patience during the process. In Jesus' name. Amen.

DAY
EIGHT

WRITE THE VISION

WRITE THE VISION

Day 8: Write the Vision
Habukkah 2:2

Then the Lord replied: "Write down the revelation and make it plain on tablets so a herald may run with it.

If ever there was a case for writing a business plan and setting SMARTER (specific, measurable, attainable, realistic, time-bound, exciting and relevant to your season) goals, this scripture is one. Success is intentional and strategic – don't expect it to happen by mere chance, without work and proper planning.

There are so many benefits to setting a solid foundation. A well written plan not only helps you and prepares you for the future, but it allows your team and partners to catch onto the vision so they can run with it.

Sometimes we embark on a journey filled with excitement at the beginning. As we begin to face obstacles, our excitement can wane somewhat.

Having a written plan to remind us of what we are working to achieve can reignite that flame that we need to keep going.

Writing things down is creating a template for our success for clarity, inspiration, effective execution and succession planning.

When you write things down and are able to reflect on what worked and what didn't at the end of a year, it provides a sense of awareness. You see clearly what you've accomplished and what you didn't. It also gives you knowledge of what needs tweaking and improvement, what you need to scrap and the elements you need to retain.

Take the time that is necessary to write your plans so that you can measure your growth. What gets measured gets managed.

Prayer: Faithful God, I pray for your wisdom in my approach to business. Remind me to always have a plan for my ventures. Keep me grounded in your word that reminds me to write the vision and make it plain. In Jesus' name. Amen.

DAY
NINE

MY DAYS HAVE BEEN WRITTEN

MY DAYS HAVE BEEN WRITTEN

Day 9: My Days Have Been Written
Psalm 139:16

Your eyes saw my unformed body; all the days ordained for me were written in your book before one of them came to be.

A fetus stays in its mother's womb for nine months before it is time to make its grand entry into the world. During this time, the psychological and physiological bond between mother and fetus is profound. She supplies all that is necessary for her unborn child to be nurtured whilst in the womb.

Except what is visible via ultra-sound, the mother can only imagine what her baby actually looks like before it is born.

When the child is born, another maternal instinct comes to the forefront. She is ready and willing to protect her baby at all costs.

But God sees us all and knows everything about before we were born, even while being just a fetus. Not only that, all our days have already been recorded. God has the total picture of what our lives will turn out to be.

Since he created us, knows everything about us and has a great plan for us, then we know that in his wisdom, he will continue to favor us to achieve beyond what we could imagine. In 1 Corinthians 2:9 we are reminded that, "What no eye has seen, what no ear has heard, and what no human mind has conceived" the things God has prepared for those who love him.

Because God has the blue print for our lives, it means he has ultimate control. We are therefore to trust his hand as he leads like the good Father he is. This is great news for us as entrepreneurs.

The anxious moments that may accompany the territory can be reduced by resting with confidence in the assurance that God knows all about you and that he wants you to excel. As a good Father, he has only great expectations of you.

Trust the all-knowing God to guide you in your pursuit of success.

Prayer: Omnipresent God, I give thanks that you are all knowing. I trust you that I can lay my fears and concerns at your feet. I know my life is in your hands. Hold me firmly and allow me to always trust your movements in my life. In Jesus' name. Amen.

DAY
TEN

STOP BEING ANXIOUS

STOP BEING ANXIOUS

Day 10: Stop Being Anxious
Philippians 4:6

Do not be anxious about anything, but in every situation, by prayer and petition, with thanksgiving, present your requests to God.

How many times have you been faced with a challenge that, from your point of view, compares in magnitude only to Mount Everest? You think to yourself, there can't possibly be any way out. In the midst of it all, you choose to be fearful, neglecting to pray and seek counsel from the one who knows it all, your Creator.

Anxiety isn't just a waste of your time, it is also unhealthy, and according to medical practitioners can lead to different types of lifestyle diseases. It makes us unproductive. Instead of problem-solve when we need to, anxiety will allow us to miss opportunities that ordinarily we would have leveraged.

There isn't anything that we can go through that will take God off guard. We should pray for

God's peace to guard our hearts and minds whenever we become anxious, as his peace surpasses all human understanding – it is unfathomable.

As Children of God, we have the mind of Christ, a mind that is free from stress and worry. As joint heirs with Jesus, we too have that gift.

When you choose faith over fear and foster an attitude of gratitude, you are able to position yourself to win.

Pray continuously along the way. The benefits and rewards that a life of prayer brings are unlike any other.

Prayer: Jehovah Shalom, you are my peace. Protect my mind from worry, anxiety and stress. Remind me to look to you always so that my fears will not magnify and manifest themselves into illnesses and unproductivity. I seek to focus my thoughts on you so that I can always be in a place of peace. In Jesus' name. Amen.

DAY
ELEVEN

LAYING THE FOUNDATION

LAYING THE FOUNDATION

Day 11: Laying the Foundation
Zechariah 4:9

The hands of Zerubbabel have laid the foundation of this temple; his hands will also complete it. Then you will know that the Lord Almighty has sent me to you.

In the early days of our entrepreneurial journey our excitement can overshadow the reality of what the journey will be like – the ups, the downs and everything in between. We see only the big picture, blinding us to what it will really take for our success.

The journey of a thousand miles begin with the first step. We must resist the temptation to discount the value of early beginnings. Too often we are in a hurry to get to the destination without appreciating the small and necessary steps to get there.

We must have a solid foundation to build on so that when the inevitable challenges come, we can withstand them. A solid foundation includes setting up systems to deal with all aspects of the business. As we lay each block, we get to see, little by little to the end of our vision, however long it takes. This is a time-consuming process, requiring discipline and a relentless pursuit of what God has put placed in our hearts. As God makes the provision for the vision he gives you, he will bless your efforts along the way.

The completion of your journey is a witness to the fact that you were sent by God for the season and time you are in. A time in which only you can do a particular thing because you were purposed to do it.

Make a resolve to stay the course regardless of the hurdles that may be in your way. It will mean getting the buy-in from others to support your dream, among other things.

Prayer: Dear God, you are the solid rock on which I stand. Keep me rooted and grounded in your word and the vision that you have given me. Give me the grace to always trust that you will make provision for my success. In Jesus' name. Amen.

DAY
TWELVE

GOD WILL BLESS YOU

GOD WILL BLESS YOU

Day 12: God Will Bless You
2 Corinthians 9:8

And God is able to bless you abundantly, so that in all things at all times, having all that you need, you will abound in every good work.

I remember a song we often sing as children growing up, *"All good things around us are sent from heaven above. O thank the Lord, oh thank the Lord for all His love"*. God desires only good things for us. He not only wants to bless us spiritually, but he wants to bless us with the things that we need whilst we are on earth – always.

Free your mind and take all negative thoughts captive. Thinking negatively about situations will only attract negative results. The bible reminds us that what we think is what we become; thoughts become things; as a person thinks in her or his heart, that is what she or he is.

Having an abundance mentality sets the foundation for us to not only survive but thrive. As believers, we must walk in this awareness and knowledge. It is the will of God for our lives to flourish and prosper even as our souls do.

Remind yourself of who you are in Christ; you are a precious gem, royalty and deserving of every good thing. Open your heart to receive it abundantly more than you could ever imagine.

Prayer: Abba, I thank you for you love that extends to every area of my life, even the minutest of detail. Thank you that you want all that is good for me. Keep my thoughts pure and positive as I open my heart to receive in abundance, the blessings that are assigned to me. In Jesus' name. Amen.

DAY
THIRTEEN

JUST BELIEVE

JUST BELIEVE

Day 13: Just Believe
Mark 5:36

Overhearing what they said, Jesus told them, "Don't be afraid; just believe."

Have you ever been asked what you thought was a difficult question and immediately you begin over thinking to come up with the answer? Later, you realized that it was really much ado about nothing and that the answer was really simple. We can all relate to a moment like this. It seems to be in our nature to expect that things are going to be or has to be difficult.

In one of the stories where Jesus raised Jairus' daughter and healed the woman with the issue of bleeding for twelve years, he could hear people from the crowd in chatter. No doubt they were in disbelief about whether it was possible. Overhearing, Jesus boldly told them, *"Don't be afraid; just believe."*

He is saying the same thing to us now in whatever situation we face along our entrepreneurial journey. Never mind the size of the boulders, don't worry, just trust God and fear not. Even when things aren't going according to plan and the strategies don't seem to be working out, identify other ways of doing things. Pivot as necessary but remain steadfast in your resolve to achieve.

A firm belief in what you are doing will inspire confidence that will lead to results. Put your all in what you do as you faithfully apply yourself to the tasks ahead.

Trust in the Lord with all your heart.

Prayer: Omnipotent God, allow me to increase my faith in you. I want to always trust your hand in my life and the work that you've called me to. Remove any unbelief from my heart that may hinder my progress. In Jesus' name. Amen.

DAY
FOURTEEN

THE REAL ENEMY

THE REAL ENEMY

Day 14: The Real Enemy
Ephesians 6:12

For our struggle is not against flesh and blood, but against the rulers, against the authorities, against the powers of this dark world and against the spiritual forces of evil in the heavenly realms.

Can you remember the last misunderstanding that led to an uncomfortable situation in your business? Who did you blame? What was your attitude?

We must remember that in this life we will face challenges. The real enemy is not your customers, team members, creditors, debtors or any other stake holder.

Good and evil are always at odds. Where there is light, darkness doesn't exist and darkness is uncomfortable with light.

The bible makes it clear that our struggles are not with each other but against the dark forces of this world. The next time you encounter an unwelcoming situation and you feel you should get even with the other party involved, think about it carefully. Ask God to grant you his discerning spirit so you can recognize who the real enemy is and approach the situation accordingly.

This will shift your focus so you can operate from a place of love, dealing with the situation without any personal attack. Refrain from judging as love can't exist where judgement is.

Remember, greater is He that is in you than the enemy that is lurking around in the world, trying to distract you and throw you off balance.

Prayer: Dear God, please grant me a discerning spirit so I can know when the enemy is at work. Help me to stand firm in knowing who I am in you. Remove any scale from my eyes that would prevent me from seeing your truth. In Jesus' name. Amen

DAY
FIFTEEN

BE A RIVER NOT A RESERVOIR

BE A RIVER NOT A RESERVOIR

Day 15: Be a River not a Reservoir
1 Peter 4:10

Each of you should use whatever gift you have received to serve others, as faithful stewards of God's grace in its various forms.

Give people what they want and they in turn will give you what you want. This level of thinking will allow you to approach networking events for example in a different way. Our aim is to find out how best we can add value to others instead of going in with a mentality of what can I get out of this.

The right attitude is one that fosters relationship building instead of a transactional approach.

Our gifts, treasures, skills and talents were not given to us for us. They were meant to serve others. We are merely stewards. As such, it is our responsibility to ensure we nurture them to the best of our abilities, giving them room to grow and develop to their full potential for the benefit of others.

It is in sharing these resources with others that they blossom. Everyone wins. We feel a sense of personal gratification when we extend our hand to others. Those, we serve get to experience the love of God through our actions.

That's the cycle of life; you give to others and others will pour into you, perhaps not even those you've served but somehow, someone definitely will.

Decide today to give more than you receive.

Prayer: Dear God, thank you for the many gifts, talents and resources that you have given me. Remind me that I am a steward of them and that they are intended to serve others. Remove any selfishness from my heart and let me give unconditionally. In Jesus' name. Amen.

DAY
SIXTEEN

LEARN TO GIVE THANKS

LEARN TO GIVE THANKS

Day 16: Learn to Give Thanks
Colossians 3:17

And whatever you do, whether in word or deed, do it all in the name of the Lord Jesus, giving thanks to God the Father through him.

Have you ever found yourself in a situation where everyone around you seemed to be pointing to the negative way of dealing with things? Some people are wired to see the undesirable in everything.

How many people are living a life fixated on what they don't have, what they see other people doing, or the humble beginnings they've had in life?

Our world unfortunately, is driven by feelings and emotions. This results from the fact that majority of what is broadcasted in the media has some form of negative overtone.

The productive state of mind is a renewed state of mind that challenges the status quo and reaches for the positive perspective with endless possibilities.

You should challenge yourself to shift the paradigm if you find yourself going in that downward spiral.

Learning to give thanks is simply choosing to see your glass as half full rather than half empty. Understanding that everything is working for your good despite what it may seem or feel like. Remember this, everything that happens to you helps you in the development of who you are becoming. We are all a culmination of our experiences to date. Even as you are reading this devotional, the question is how are you evolving into the best version of yourself?

Thankfulness is contagious, it has no prejudices and holds no grudge. It finds a reason to celebrate life in all of its aspects.

Today, decide to rid your mind of any negativity that might be consuming you and infuse yourself with thoughts, ideas, goals and daily activities with the practice of giving thanks. Start simply by waking up with a celebration for a new day. Continue on by appreciating all that you do have, to include the good, the bad and the unpleasant.

Learn to see things through the lens of thanksgiving and add a little kindness to everything you do. As an entrepreneur, decide to keep a gratitude journal, listing all the things that you are grateful for. When you do this, you open your heart to receive even more than what you already have.

Prayer: Dear Heavenly Father, thank you for giving me the ability to recognize your grace and mercy over my life. Remind me daily that I have reason to bless your holy name each and every day. May I be light that others may see you in me. In Jesus' name. Amen.

DAY
SEVENTEEN

ERADICATE PROCRASTINATION

ERADICATE PROCRASTINATION

Day 17: Eradicate Procrastination.
Proverbs 18:9

One who is slack in his work is brother to one who destroys.

The mind is an incubator for greatness, but can also become the cavern of immobility. The body is a beautiful creation that takes commands from the mind. If you change your mind it can and will change the trajectory of your life. You have heard it said at least a hundred times in your lifetime, that a mind is a terrible thing to waste, but so is an opportunity.

Procrastination is nothing more than being lazy because you think you have time to do something that you know should or even may need to be done right now. Or perhaps you are not lazy but you just haven't taken the time to learn how to do what you want to do and so you delay. Make a decision to find all the resources that you will need to move ahead and act.

We are all given equal time but separated by how we leverage it.

Let's do an evaluation. On this day, take an assessment of your months, weeks, and days so far, this year. How many things have you procrastinated on? What were those things and did you eventually complete them? For the things that you didn't complete, was it because you underestimated the time that it would take to get them done? Again, what you focus on, gets done.

Look at your time from the stand point of an hour glass. How much can you get accomplished with the hour that it takes for the sand to move from one section to the next. How about challenging yourself to become an ACTIONAIRE instead of a procrastinator.

Actionaires are people who take advantage of the opportunity to take action. Start asking yourself the question "WHY NOT?" as oppose to "WHY NOW"?

Change your mindset towards the things you need to get done; see them as fun steps to accomplishing your goals and watch how your life and business begin to yield the evidence and results you desire.

Prayer: Dear Lord, create in me a heart to serve you in all things. I desire to execute on a daily basis that which you have created me for. May your word be the lamp and light unto my feet that allows me to take ACTION. In Jesus' name. Amen.

DAY
EIGHTEEN

LIVE TO PRODUCE

LIVE TO PRODUCE

Day 18: Live to Produce
Genesis 1:26- 28

Then God said, "Let us make mankind in our image, in our likeness, so that they may rule over the fish in the sea and the birds in the sky, over the livestock and all the wild animals,[a] *and over all the creatures that move along the ground." So God created mankind in his own image, in the image of God he created them; male and female he created them. God blessed them and said to them, "Be fruitful and increase in number; fill the earth and subdue it. Rule over the fish in the sea and the birds in the sky and over every living creature that moves on the ground.*

I (Vernet) have always wondered why we were given the ability to have dominion over the entire earth. Why did God (intentionally vs just randomly) say here take everything I've created, it's yours to dominate? Why not just say, here you can use these things, but ask me first before you do?

God wants us to live to produce. If you pay special attention to the words he uses in the scripture, he points out that he has made humans in his own image. That is powerful.

We were created to bring him glory by doing exactly what he has already intended for us to do. He said be fruitful, multiple and replenish the earth. As his creation, we are to 'Live to Produce' as he avowed us to do.

What do your actions proclaim? Are you living as a child of the King? Are you making a difference in the earth? If you doubt that you are, it's time to make a shift because to do otherwise is to live beneath your potential.

Search God's word to see what it says about you. How are you living to produce and making a productive impact in the lives of others?

Remember this, when we know better, we do better, become better and are better.

Prayer: Jehovah Jireh, you have been my provider all of my days. I thank you for your provision and protection over my family and the community that I serve. Teach me O Lord to be a good resource to others in all things. I decrease that you may increase in and through me. In Jesus' name. Amen.

DAY
NINETEEN

MAXIMIZE YOUR TIME

MAXIMIZE YOUR TIME

Day 19: Maximize Your Time
Psalm 90:12

Teach us to number our days, that we may gain a heart of wisdom.

How are you investing your time? Do you find that you take it for granted? Are you constantly taking on new projects to fill your day with or are you still in the rut of doing the same things day in and day out?

You have to understand that time is the one commodity that you can't get back - that moment that just passed you by, you will never get that moment again, so don't waste time, instead invest your time in doing things that you really want to do and that you have been purposed to do.

Every year there is something that occurs; it always happens without fail. You want to know what that thing is? Time keeps moving forward! Have you noticed that it never stands still for anyone? Can you believe that time is not a respecter of persons, nationality, race, creed, gender, financial or economic status? Wow, so if we are all equal in the 24 hours that we get in a day, shouldn't we seek to maximize our time?

Do you want to know the difference between YOU and OUR??? It's simple, from one perspective it's missing the R which connotes responsibility, while on the other hand it's missing the Y which places the onus on everyone from a collective stand point.

1. YOU should maximize your time-responsibility set and accepted.
2. WE should maximize OUR time.

Before we can think collectively and move as a unit in any endeavor, we must first place the responsibility on ourselves and start asking the question: What am I going to do about it? How do I plan to do it? When do you expect to get it done? Once you establish that, it now becomes YOUR plan.

Prayer: God my father, thank you for always watching over me and redeeming the time for my sake. What the enemy thought for evil you have turned around for my good time after time. I thank you for the wisdom and insight to discern my priorities. In Jesus' name. Amen.

DAY
TWENTY

BE DILIGENT IN ALL THINGS

BE DILIGENT IN ALL THINGS

Day 20: Be Diligent in all Things
Proverbs 1 2:24

Diligent hands will rule, but laziness ends in forced labor.

He that is diligent in his affairs will always reap the benefits of his labor. This brings to mind the saying, *'if you don't work, then you don't eat'*. In the streets, they would say your level of hustle will determine your level of success.

In the marketing arena, he who is first to present is the owner of the idea or concept. In the business space, the one who creates opportunity is the boss. In the financial domain, the borrower will always be subject to the demand of the lender. In the entrepreneurial space, the brand that stands out the strongest and produces the most value is king.

The underlying theme is to put in the work, and be prudent in all things. A farmer sets out to reap a harvest before the crop is ever laid in the ground, because he is diligent in all his ways. He tends to the soil, prepares it to receive the seed, nurtures it with proper nutrients and guards it from whatever may keep it from producing the crop that the seed was designed to produce.

We can learn a lot from the methodologies of the farmer. What are you doing to be diligent in every area of your life? How can a simple and subtle change, shift the trajectory of your success? One thing is certain it's that proper execution of knowledge applied can yield exponential growth.

Being diligent will lead to a life changing experience. It has proven to be a habit, and principle that highly successful individuals practice.

Prayer: Abba Father, you are my beginning and my end. My desire is to serve you all the days of my life. With everything that is within me, I will bless your holy name. May you always get the best of my labor, both in word and in deed. Search my heart O lord that it may be pure. In Jesus' name. Amen.

DAY
TWENTY-ONE

TRUST BUT VERIFY

TRUST BUT VERIFY

Day 21: Trust but Verify
1 Thessalonians 5:21

But test them all; hold on to what is good.

Life offer lessons in everything it has to offer to us. A key principle that highly productive people use in life as a strategy is, 'trust but verify'. This is done by doing research and observing before accepting a principle or fact as truth.

In academia, you must have a source to validate your statements and or viewpoints before you make any pronouncements. In business, your vision statement must be backed by actions. In the medical field, medicine should have proper research and development prior to being released to the market.

Who goes to the dentist without doing their research first to know the past performance of such professional? Who puts money into investments without checking its track record or history? What parent allows their children to go to a school without first checking its ratings and credibility?

At the end of the day, identify that which is good about yourself and present that on a daily basis.

Two of my favorite words which I live by are truth and transparency. When you find, yourself walking in the character of these traits, life becomes extremely simple. Most people can't fathom a life of truth and transparency because they are so accustomed to being guarded. This guardedness may be a barrier of protection resulting from years of bitterness and pain. But, it can be reversed simply by your decision to let it go and to move forward.

Make a decision to walk in transparency in all your endeavors so that others will get to know like and trust you.

Prayer: Abba father, you are my beginning and my end. My desire is to serve you all the days of my life. With everything that is within me, I will bless your holy name. May you always get the best of my labor, both in word and in deed. Search my heart O lord that it may be pure. In Jesus' name. Amen.

DAY
TWENTY-TWO

DO THE WORK

DO THE WORK

Day 22: Do the Work
Psalm 128:2

You will eat the fruit of your labor; blessings and prosperity will be yours.

Anything worth having is worth working for! This statement has so much value that it should be etched on gold bars everywhere and displayed for all to see.

There is just something about having to work for what you want and to seeing it make a distinctive difference in the lives of people. As a child, I appreciated gifts given to me; but anything I physically worked for, I cherished!

In a passage of scripture in Genesis, God told man that he would have to live from the 'sweat of his brow'; he spoke to women, telling them they would have to go through the 'pain of child bearing'.

The love that a mother has for her child is so intense, that they are practically inseparable. Why? Because she is the one who puts in the work of carrying that baby to term. Not only does she have to care for herself, but she also has to be considerate of the baby she is carrying. How she eats, sleeps, exercises and carries herself, all play an important part in birthing a healthy baby.

Imagine having to work for nine months before being able to receive your pay (prize). Isn't that what a mother goes through? Although a far-reaching analogy, it highlights the importance of doing the work.

When you do the work, you can expect a return! Ask yourself, "Am I putting in the amount of time, effort and energy necessary to achieve success?" If not, you may realize that you don't have the results you desire. And even if you are experiencing success, there is so much more you can accomplish.

Start your success journey by acknowledging where you are and by putting in the work necessary for your growth.

Prayer: El Elyon, thank you for being both my protector and provider, it is because of you, that I have strength to do the work. Teach my hands O Lord to glorify you, my mouth to speak of your goodness and my heart to follow your wisdom each and every day. In Jesus' name. Amen.

DAY
TWENTY- THREE

BE ANXIOUS FOR NOTHING

BE ANXIOUS FOR NOTHING

Day 23: Be Anxious for Nothing
Jeremiah 17:7-9

But blessed is the one who trusts in the Lord, whose confidence is in him. They will be like a tree planted by the water that sends out its roots by the stream. It does not fear when heat comes; its leaves are always green. It has no worries in a year of drought and never fails to bear fruit." The heart is deceitful above all things and beyond cure. Who can understand it?

As leaders, it is extremely important that we take to carefully analyze and make proper judgement when doing things. Oftentimes we can get caught up in the rat race of getting things done, that we forget the adage, 'patience is a virtue'. We are instructed to be anxious for nothing, but in this fast-paced world that we live in, it takes discipline to maintain this instruction.

Currently more than 40 million Americans over the age of 18 are suffering from chronic anxiety. Emotional disorders and prescriptions drugs to correct such issues are on the rise, but there is an answer to this epidemic. The key is for humanity to allow itself to collide with divinity.

Learning how to be still and know that GOD is the source of our strength enables all believers, particularly those in business, to live a worry free, stress free and care free life.

We were not built to carry the burden of the world on our shoulders, nor were we built to mistreat our mind, body and souls. Think about what makes an individual anxious, stressed or depressed. It is often caused by things that are out of their control.

The cure is in a few simple words – Let go and let GOD!

Read this simple scripture found in Philippians 4:6-7, "Do not be anxious about anything, but in every situation, by prayer and petition, with thanksgiving, present your requests to God. And the peace of God, which transcends all understanding, will guard your hearts and your minds in Christ Jesus."

As you read, meditate on the words and let them slowly take the emotions away that are causing you to feel anxious.

Prayer: Jehovah Shalom, You are the Lord of peace and I thank you for keeping me in my right state of mind. No weapon formed against me shall prosper and I will give no room for the enemy to rule my thoughts. Lord I cast my cares upon you, as I know you care for me. In Jesus' name. Amen.

DAY
TWENTY-FOUR

THE LAW OF SOWING & REAPING

THE LAW OF SOWING & REAPING

Day 24: The Law of Sowing and Reaping
Genesis 26:12

Isaac planted crops in that land and the same year reaped a hundredfold, because the Lord blessed him.

This practical, yet powerful law teaches us the importance of our daily actions. In life, every action has a consequence. We are all a culmination of the experiences that we have had to date. Every thought, intent and action in our past bears fruit to our present and springboards into our future.

The law of sowing and reaping can be found in every area of life to include mental, physical, spiritual and relational. The seeds that are sown are planted, nurtured and eventually bear fruit.

This is no less true when it comes to our finances so it is a relevant analogy to make the point. The principle of sowing and reaping is like unto investing in a bank or stocks, but with a strange exchange. Banks give loans with the intent of making money. People invest in stocks with the intent of increasing their bottom line over time.

The key is to recognize the principles found within this law. Galatians 6:7 states *"Do not be deceived, God is not mocked; for whatever a man sows, this he will also reap."*

First, we must take away that there is no prejudice associated with God's law. What God says is true for anyone who follows it. This is applicable to those who believe and even to those that don't.

Secondly, we should get a better understanding of the adage *'You reap what you sow.'* What you put out into the atmosphere will return to you. When you sow a seed, recognize that it will take time to develop, but when it does it reproduces after its own kind so you can harvest.

Make a conscious decision to sow good seeds so your harvest will be plentiful.

Prayer: Jehovah Jireh, I place my trust in you with all that I have. When you speak, my desire is to execute that which you have spoken. My desire is to sow the seeds of love, goodness and the examples that you modeled before me that I may live a quiet and peaceable life. In Jesus' name. Amen.

DAY
TWENTY- FIVE

BEWARE OF THE THIEF OF
PROCRASTINATION

BEWARE OF PROCRASTINATION

Day 25: Beware of Procrastination
Ecclesiastes 11:4

Whoever watches the wind will not plant; whoever looks at the clouds will not reap.

Love is an action word! Christ came that we might have life and it more abundantly. God the Father sent his son to die for our sins, because he LOVES us so much. Notice in this statement that God didn't hesitate to offer up His only begotten son when there was a problem. He didn't say that I have this all under control and I will take my sweet time to get it done.

Although God is omnipotent and is in control of everything, He knows that procrastination is an enemy and thief of successful outcomes.

Most people procrastinate because they don't have a sense of time. They believe that they can accomplish the task at hand whenever and however their hearts desire. With this mentality, nothing actually gets accomplished. Therefore, procrastination is the thief of both time and accomplishment.

As productive individuals, we cannot afford to make excuses for inactivity or non-productive behavior. The scriptures give us an example in this passage *"Faith without works is dead."* What does this mean? You can have the faith to do something, but if you don't put action to your faith then it remains stagnant and eventually dies.

Unfortunately, when we believe that we have time to accomplish things we put it off until it time 'creeps' up on us unaware; we waste time until we are out of time.

Let us be aware of the thief of time, i.e. procrastination and not let it rob us of our victories.

Prayer: Heavenly Father, there is no one like you in all the earth. I respect and appreciate you and your infinite wisdom. It is my duty to produce and bring forth fruit, from that which you have placed in my hands. My prayer is that I will make you proud on a daily basis. May I never take your love for granted. In Jesus' name. Amen.

DAY
TWENTY-SIX

LEARN FROM THE ANT

LEARN FROM THE ANT

Day 26: Learn From the Ant
Proverbs 6:6-11

Go to the ant, you sluggard; consider its ways and be wise! It has no commander, no overseer or ruler, yet it stores its provisions in summer and gathers its food at harvest. How long will you lie there, you sluggard? When will you get up from your sleep? A little sleep, a little slumber, a little folding of the hands to rest— and poverty will come on you like a thief and scarcity like an armed man.

When we take heed to our environment, everything around us comes alive. You can learn a lot from simply observing nature and your surroundings.

Believe it or not, there is LIFE and energy in all that we do! The universe reacts and responds to our thoughts and ideas, but more importantly to the actions we take while executing what we believe. That's how God intended it.

Let's look at the ANT in this passage. Wisdom is the principled thing. With all your getting (of wisdom), it is imperative to get understanding. The ant is a wonderful example of how we all need to implement strategic planning and prioritization in our lives and business. Do you have the foresight to plan in the winter so that you can harvest in the summer? Are you willing to do the uncommon so that you can make a long-term impact? The ant shows us how to shift the paradigm so that we can be significant while being successful.

Success is what you can accomplish for yourself versus significance, which is what you are able to influence others to accomplish.

Follow these six steps to achieve success.

1. Establish A Routine
2. Be Organized
3. Make Deadlines
4. Take Small Breaks
5. Stay Motivated
6. Know Yourself

As you aim for success, remember that it is about impact and significance.

Prayer: Heavenly Father, Open the eyes of my heart and understanding that I may serve you and your people all of my days. I thank you for the wisdom to know when to act and when to listen. Thank you for loving me and entrusting me with your love, knowledge, wisdom and grace. In Jesus' name. Amen.

DAY
TWENTY- SEVEN

TAPPING INTO YOUR INNER
STRENGTH

TAPPING INTO YOUR INNER STRENGTH

Day 27: Tapping into Your Inner Strength
Psalm 105:24

The Lord made his people very fruitful; he made them too numerous for their foes.

Why are we so focused on our weaknesses that we forget about our strengths? Society wants us to pay attention to the things that TRULY don't matter. Things like: what we don't have, who we are not, and what others are doing.

Are you familiar with the microscope or magnifying glass? Their function is to make big or enlarge something that is small; to help what is normally unseen with the common eye visible.

Be challenged today to amplify your thinking to a higher frequency to acknowledge and harness your inner strength.

God blessed every one of us with the same measure of faith in the beginning, but how we move forward and what we do with that faith is determined by our perception of our faith.

Do you believe in yourself? Are you willing to step out on your faith (in your belief in you through Christ)? What's stopping you from seeing it through? These simple yet thought-provoking questions will enable you to tap into your inner strength.

1 John 4:4 says *You, dear children, are from God and have overcome them, because the one who is in you is greater than the one who is in the world.*

This passage reminds us of who we are and who is truly in control.

Once you begin to fully leverage the power within, there is no limit to what you can accomplish through Christ.

Channel your inner peace and start tapping into your inner strength today. You will be surprised at the result that you will achieve in doing so.

Prayer: Heavenly Father, Open the eyes of my heart and understanding that I may serve you and your people all of my days. I thank you for the wisdom to know when to act and when to listen. Thank you for loving me and entrusting me with your love, knowledge, wisdom and grace. In Jesus' name. Amen.

DAY
TWENTY-EIGHT

STAY FOCUSED

STAY FOCUSED

Day 28: Stay Focused
Proverbs 4:25-27

Let your eyes look straight ahead; fix your gaze directly before you. Give careful thought to the[a] paths for your feet and be steadfast in all your ways. Do not turn to the right or the left; keep your foot from evil.

It is often said that if you follow a man's treasure it will lead you to his heart. What you focus on actually gets magnified and managed. Staying focused is so important because, *"As a man thinketh in his heart so is he."* Whatever you think, ponder or focus on is what you actually become.

Stop giving attention to things that really don't matter. This is majoring in the minor. Many people waste time placing emphasis on things that aren't going to help them develop in life.

In this passage, we are instructed to look forward, not keep looking back, left or right. It behooves you to look ahead to what is before you. How many of us are violating this principle daily?

Establishing a daily routine accompanied by proper planning can be a great help in increasing our focus. If it's your health, then make sure what you are eating is aligned to your desired outcome. If it is your finance, then make sure that you are saving and investing to grow your net worth. If it is your relationships, then make sure you are paying attention to your significant other and the things that make them joyful and appreciated. If it's your future, then you must plan and prepare for it.

Lastly, if you are going to be focused, then you are going to have remove distractions from your life. In other words, remove your foot from evil and stay away from the bright, shiny objects.

Prayer: Abba Father, thank you for giving me the wisdom to keep my mind stayed on you. May you be my ultimate focus and what I measure my life by. Use me for your service. In Jesus' name. Amen.

DAY
TWENTY-NINE

THE SOURCE OF ALL PRODUCTIVITY

THE SOURCE OF ALL PRODUCTIVITY

Day 29: The Source of all Productivity
Deuteronomy 8:18

But remember the Lord your God, for it is he who gives you the ability to produce wealth, and so confirms his covenant, which he swore to your ancestors, as it is today.

We were created to produce and bring glory to God. This scripture places us in remembrance of our why. Despite our lineage, we are reminded that it is God who gave us the power to get wealth and do whatever we are doing.

God shows us the purpose for him giving us power, wealth and health. It is not to be for selfish gain, or bragging rights, but to establish his covenant which was spoken years before we ever existed.

We need to place God first because He is the source of all our productivity yield. Nothing is impossible with God and nothing is possible without God. This is truth. If we lean on, trust and depend on God, we cannot, and will not be disappointed.

There is none like our God, now and forever more; he is worthy of all of our praise, honor and glory.

How do you describe the multiple blessings that God has bestowed upon your life, knowing that he is our source and strength?

As our Jehovah Jireh, God has already provided all we need for our success – we only need to look to Him.

Prayer: Jehovah, teach me to appreciate your ways. Put me in remembrance of your word that I may know the promises you have for me. In Jesus' name. Amen.

DAY
THIRTY

RUN YOUR RACE

RUN YOUR RACE

Day 30: Run Your Race
1 Corinthians 9:24

Do you not know that in a race all the runners run, but only one gets the prize? Run in such a way as to get the prize.

We are all in the race of life, but each have different destinations. Some of us are on a sprint to get to our destinations, while others are running a marathon to reach that same end goal. We will meet individuals along our journey who are in different races. No two race is the exactly the same.

Our goal should be to run and complete the race that was established for us. Don't compare your race to someone else's, as they weren't built to handle or go through what you were equipped to accomplish and vice versa.

Appreciate the path, pattern and points of interest in your race because they have made you into who you are today. Believe that what is for you is for you, no matter what comes your way. The obstacles and boundaries that you encounter are there to help you determine if you want it badly enough. No one starts a race with the intent to fall out, but somewhere along the line they get sidetracked and forget what the goal was in the first place.

Stay in your lane and on your course until you cross that finish line. The prize is ahead so don't stop until you finished.

Philippians 3:14, reminds us "I press on toward the goal to win the prize for which God has called me heavenward in Christ Jesus.

What are you pressing towards? Don't stop running your race my friend!

Prayer: Lord, you are good and your mercy endureth forever. Thank you for opening the doors that only you could open and for closing those that needed to be closed. I place my trust in you. In Jesus' name. Amen.

DAY
THIRTY- ONE

WALK IN INTEGRITY

WALK IN INTEGRITY

Day 31: Walk in Integrity
Proverbs 20:7

The righteous lead blameless lives; blessed are their children after them.

One of the greatest things that a person can do for his family is to walk upright with integrity before God and others. Having a good name is worth more that silver, gold or riches. Never short change yourself in fear of what others may think of you. Give them the thoughts that they should think through your actions.

When integrity is the focus, you won't have to worry about the perception of others. Stand for what is right and make no excuse. Proverbs 18:24 says "One who has unreliable friends soon comes to ruin, but there is a friend who sticks closer than a brother.

Speak life and walk in it. Here is a great acronym that I picked up from the military Airforce Major Ronald Frantz on INTEGRITY:

"I" - initiative. Take the initiative to do the right thing even when no one else will know.

"N" - nurture. Nurture others through the quality of your actions even when no one else will know.

"T" - teamwork. Teamwork is service before self even when no one else will know.

"E" - excellence. Excellence in all we do even when no one else will know.

"G" - giving. Giving 110 percent even when no one else will know.

"R" - respect. Respect each other even when no one else will know.

"I" - intelligence. Be intelligent by knowing your job better than anyone, even when no one else will know.

"T" - true. Be true to the best that's in you even when no one else will know.

"Y" - you. You and I can make a difference even when no one else will know.

As you pursue your entrepreneurial endeavors, remember that your integrity is worth more than any financial gain you will ever receive.

Prayer: Dear God, thank you for giving me the courage to speak and live out your word. You lead and I will continue to follow. In Jesus' name. Amen.

Authors Bio's

Dr. Vernet A. Joseph Bio

Dr. Vernet A. Joseph is America's #1 Potential, Passion & Productivity Speaker, Strategist & Consultant. An award winning serial entrepreneur, and bestselling author of 5 books, Dr. Vernet is also a Veteran Transition Expert. He's also the Founder and CEO of Live To Produce Enterprises, LLC, President of Gigaré Lifestyle Magazine, and Radio Host of "Productivity 360 with Dr. V," and Co-host of "Relationships 3D."

An international thought leader, international speaker, Dr. Vernet retired from the U.S. Army as a CW4 after 20 years of highly decorated/combat service. In the past decade, Dr. Vernet has trained millions of people in over 50 countries on 4 different continents.

One of the most requested Business Strategists, Dr. Vernet helps entrepreneurs and business owners maximize their productivity. His national recognition includes: one of the top 40 Productivity Experts to follow on Twitter, Executive Professional of the Year, HERO of Women's Entrepreneurs of America, Black Wall

Street Phoenix Arizona Entrepreneur of the Year, National Statesmen, and he was recently named a World Civility Ambassador by I Change Nations and the Golden Rule.

A devoted husband to his wife, Dr. Lynette Joseph for over 20 years, he's also a dedicated father to his beautiful daughters Dominique and Renee. Dr. Vernet is an Honorary HERO Spokesperson for the Women Entrepreneurs of America Inc., Demonstrated Master Logistician by the International Society of Logistics Engineers, Logistics Transformation & Change Management College and the Army Logistics University Sponsored by Pennsylvania State University to name a few.

Heneka Watkis-Porter Bio

Heneka Watkis-Porter is a serial-entrepreneur, author, speaker, and podcaster. She wakes up every day with a grateful heart as she lives her purpose of "life transformation through inspiration". She is the founder/CEO of Patwa Culcha International, the company that owns the authentic Jamaica clothing brand, Patwa Apparel.

Heneka is the Host/Creator of The Entrepreneurial You podcast. She is also the creator of the Caribbean's first Virtual Conference and Expo - The Entrepreneurial You Virtual SME Conference & Expo. She is the host of Leadercast events in Jamaica.

Heneka sees her business as a means to an end rather than an end in itself. She enjoys sharing her entrepreneurial experience to help empower the lives of persons with a desire to become entrepreneurs through podcasting, speaking and her books.

Heneka is an Ambassador for the Governor General of Jamaica's I Believe Initiative. She loves to travel and connect with people from around the world.

www.ingramcontent.com/pod-product-compliance
Lightning Source LLC
Chambersburg PA
CBHW021240090426

42740CB00006B/614